Ebay Ultimate Gold Rush, A Home Base Business And Self Employment

Quality Information At Your Door Step

DANIEL N. NNERDY

DISCLAIMER:

While all attempts have been made to verify information provided in this publication, neither the author nor the publisher assumes any responsibility for errors, omissions, or contrary interpretation of the subject matter herein.

This publication is not intended for use as a source of legal or accounting advice. The publisher and author wants to stress that the information contained herein may be subject to varying state and/or local laws or regulations. All users are advised to determine what state and/or local laws or regulations may apply to the user's particular business.

The purchaser or reader of this publication assumes all responsibility for the use of these materials and information. The author and publisher assume no responsibility or liability whatsoever on the behalf of any purchaser or reader of these materials. Results are not typical. Your results may vary. The author and publisher make no claims about obtaining any results whatsoever. Where specific figures are quoted from individuals there is no guarantee you will have similar results. This publication is full of useful information which has the potential to greatly enhance your personal situation as it has to others worldwide. We encourage you to get started reading today.

Dedication

To my humble wife Mrs. Victoria Chizoma Nnerdy, I wish her more years ahead.

.

CONTENTS

Daniel N. Nnerdy

ACKNOWLADGEMENTS

My acknowledgements to everyone who's reading this book now.

1 JOINING EBAY

Joining eBay is easy to do. This article has a look at how to join eBay, what eBay is, and why the internet is the modern marketplace and how to join through a safe link. Many people hear the amazing stories of growth of online companies like Google (now worth $450 Billion) and eBay and not being very online aware ask me the question, but how can these companies be worth that much how? What do they do? Surely that's just all hype? This is a hangover from the dot.com bubble burst. Many people heard of these flash in the pan internet companies worth millions one night and nothing the next. So many people still think the internet doesn't have any commercial footing.

Nothing could be further from the truth. In any new industry there has always been the same pattern - a new product is discover or becomes useful, every man and his dog sees the opportunity and jumps on the gold rush, one or two companies actually come to dominate the market. This pattern has been repeated again and again - take oil - originally thousands of small companies but after the original bubble burst, Standard Oil emerged to dominate the market. Computers - Microsoft, Automobiles - the big three - Ford, GM, Chrysler, (now worth less combined than Google), search engines - Google and yahoo.

EBay is and currently remains, and I predict is high likely to remain the number internet auction site. Millions of items every day are put up for auction and eBay makes its income off listing fees and taking a cut of the final sale price. Whilst there are other auctions sites that have cheaper rates, eBay continues to dominate the market because it attracts the most number of buyers due to a combination of brand recognition, smart affiliate marketing, huge market share, ease of use, and good security protections in place.

EBay is a buyers dream with just about everything available for sale (other than animals - an opening for a smart programmer to start an online animal exchange - consider the amount of cattle that changes hands in the USA each day, but back to the topic), and for sale at hugely discounted rates.

If you have shopping to do up with a user name and a password. Make sure your username is something you a happy with as it will be your name on eBay; I don't recommend you eBay can make a limited budget go a long way. Further although a lot of second hand items are sold on eBay, it's not just a place of other peoples unwanted junk, a huge quantity of the items for sale are brand new and often better than the shops.

Take my wife's eBay business for example, selling baby clothes - unlike your local shop, these clothes are still fresh in the original plastic wrapper straight from the factory, not tried on or handled by hundreds of potential shoppers with a variety of hygiene levels as is the case in a retail store.

Joining eBay just requires clicking on a link to eBay. Click on a banner you trust as some criminals have set up copycat eBay sites. Click on the banner which takes you straight to eBay and a sign up page, I've provided some links below. Here you will need to come use your real name and keep your password safe.

EBay will want to verify you are who you say you are so will need a postal address (one account per address) and will receive a letter in the mail from eBay with instructions to on how to verify you are who you say you are.

An important concept on eBay is your rating. People can leave a positive or negative comment about their dealings with you. This is a reflection on your character and your behavior on eBay. Fail to go through with a winning auction bid, give a false description of a product, fail to deliver a product and you can expect a negative rating. Good transactions result in positive ratings.

Of course though although most fellow ebayers are nice you get the one customer that you can't please no matter what you do, that's just life, very few people on eBay keep a 100% rating and this would be unrealistic to expect given human nature.

To quickly build a rating in a day buy some eBooks and the like, you can get them cheap; there are even items for 1 cent. Buying some of these items can quickly and cheaply raise your rating to a level where others are more likely to be happy to do business with you.

Although the format of eBay can be a bit scary at first after a week or two you make get an incurable addiction and become an eBay addict, especially when you realize what you saved compared to retail price.

2 HOW TO GET STARTED WITH EBAY

You probably heard it - the fastest way to earn extra money online is to sell on eBay. You can start right now, today, and in 3 days be paid online for items you sell. All you need is to register at the eBay site, read their tutorial and get started selling items you have around the house. EBay is a 70 billion dollar a year industry giant and they are dependent on entrepreneurs to make that business figure grow.

Entrepreneurs mean people like me and you. In 2005, the number of people making money from working on eBay increased by 68%. As eBay researched, over 724,000 million people either make a full time or a supplemental income from working eBay. And another 1.5 million say that eBay gives them additional income throughout the year.

So there are many ways to get started on eBay for an extra income.

Lots of people make a few extra dollars while others are making a fortune. EBay or any business you get into online or in a physical business location has the potential to make money. The great thing about online businesses is it usually costs a lot less to get started than opining a brick and mortar store. For instance, getting started selling on eBay doesn't cost anything. You only pay fees when you run an eBay auction ad. Lots of people succeed in business and a lot fail. Your success or failure will partially depend on how well you prepare, how much you study and how much energy you put into the project.

The main thing is to get a plan and work the plan. You should make it a weekly routine to research on eBay which items are selling like crazy and think about the question whether you might sell them as well. Anyway gather up some income products from around your home, your relatives, garage sales, thrift stores, big lots or consignment shops. Invest a set amount, say $200. Make sure that you get items that are useful or entertaining and that provide a quick turn over.

The way to do that is to think about your own buying habits. Would you purchase this item if you saw it advertised, does it appeal to a mass market; is it a niche product people might be willing to purchase? What you want are items that you can pick up for very little money and that you can put up on eBay for a small price and, thereby, create an immediate cash flow.

At first, you will want to return almost all your profits back into purchasing some more items to sell. You will do this until you have a comfortable amount of money invested in your business and then you will have set up your own profit stream.

To get your items ready to market what you need to do is to take a quality digital photo of the item from different angles. For smaller items, you should use a whiteboard backdrop to get the maximum amount of light with few reflections. For larger items, outside shots work well, just have the sun behind your back when taking the picture.

You also need to write up a very good description of your item and do not try to hide any imperfections. Once more: it will be always helpful to research on eBay, what others are doing and how they are doing. You don't have to reinvent the wheel, but don't just copy a good sales letter or listing, let it be an inspiration for you. Point out the usefulness and benefits of your item as well. A description that is fair and honest will result in much better comments received in eBay feedback.

You can open a starting seller's eBay store a monthly fee and have about five pages to sell your items. You also receive a free month when you start your store, so you can get a feel for how it all works. You will have to pay eBay for their sale fees which amount to an insertion fee and a selling fee. Please take this into consideration when fixing your price.

A eBay store is a very effective way to display your items, drive traffic to a website, or to display a couple of your best items in eBay auctions and get people to visit your other items through your store listing on your auction websites. After you sell an item, you will be eligible for "feedback."

This is where the buyer makes comments about your service, your responsiveness to email questions, and general comments about how it was interact with you as a seller of eBay items. You want this to be 100% or as close as possible to it.

If there is a dispute on any item, you will try to work it out and make sure that the buyer is satisfied within your own selling descriptions. You want return customers and you want others that will check your feedback section to be sure to find good comments about your service.

A good feedback is the most important thing on eBay for you as a seller, it determines your success! The feedback enables those who have not conducted business with you to know your track record and feel more confident that they will have a good buying experience with your company or store. EBay will only continue to grow as more and more people make money with them, so why not capitalize on this easy to do program. Go where the people are looking to buy...that is EBAY right now!

3 THE EASIEST WAY TO MAKE MONEY ONLINE TODAY

Did you know that most people who make big money on the net do so by selling dubious money-making schemes to others? And they seem to get better at it every day. They have mastered the art of using enticing headlines that grab you by the neck and pull in sales even from spam.

Make no mistake about it, these guys know human nature and use their knowledge to the maximum.

This gives an honest person like you and me no chance at all. Little wonder that so many of us have lost so much money online by ordering "guaranteed money-making schemes" that never worked This article is not supposed to discourage you or kill your dreams of making it big online. The aim here is to give you the facts.

Facts that will help you decide on a course of action that will change your online fortunes.

The facts are that there are thousands of people making money online.

This is a fact that the hype and scum artistes have cashed in on to sell their schemes, which benefit nobody else but themselves. The facts are that vast majorities of people who make money online, genuinely, make it using well-known web sites.

So while your efforts to be original and unique are appreciated, would it not be a better idea to find a proven, easy way to make money online?

You can then use your profits to finance all the other adventures you have in mind, and your experiences to help you succeed much more easily with project number two. You would naturally want to get the information to succeed from an expert. An expert being somebody who has made money from the particular well-known site you have chosen to go with.

Let us say that you make the wise decision to zero in on the single site that has had the highest number of publicized cases of people who have actually made money. Real people with real names and addresses. The site of course is eBay.

You would naturally want to get your information from an eBay expert.

Actually there is such a person. Somebody who has made over $350,000 in sales, in less than one year, working part-time. Somebody who has successfully auctioned a wide variety of items like:

• Wide screen TV sets

• Wedding dresses

• DVD players

• Garden ornaments

• Jewelry

• Designer goods

• VCRs

• Tools

• Binoculars

• Cars and even information products...

By simply understanding and knowing what you are doing, you can be very successful doing your online business through eBay auctions. The traffic on eBay is massive, check out the figures for yourself at any source you trust. eBay.com has a staggering 10 million items on sale at any point in time. The site gets 1.5 billion auction page views each month.

This is the key that makes it so easy for ordinary people to make money on eBay. It is simply a matter of taking your products to where the customers are waiting for it. But you need to know what you are doing. It all boils down to getting the formula to maximize your auction effectiveness.

4 INCOME POSSIBILITIES ON EBAY

If you've ever read an article about eBay, you will have seen the kinds of incomes people make - it isn't unusual to hear of people making thousands of dollars per month on eBay.

Next time you're on eBay, take a look at how many PowerSellers there are: you'll find quite a few. Now consider that every single one of one of them must be making at least $1,000 per month, as that's eBay's requirement for becoming a PowerSeller.

Silver PowerSellers make at least $3,000 each month, while Gold

PowerSellers make more than $10,000, and the Platinum level is $25,000. The top ranking is Titanium PowerSellers, and to qualify you must make at least $150,000 in sales every month!

The fact that these people exist gives you some idea of the income possibilities here. Most of them never set out to even set up a business on eBay - they simply started selling a few things, and then kept going. There are plenty of people whose full-time job is selling things on eBay, and some of them have been doing it for years now. Can you imagine that?

Once they've bought the stock, everything else is pretty much pure profit for these people - they don't need to pay for any business premises, staff, or anything else.

There are multi-million dollar businesses making less in actual profit than eBay PowerSellers do...

Even if you don't want to quit your job and really go for it, you can still use eBay to make a significant second income. You can pack up orders during the week and take them down to the post office for delivery each Saturday.

There are few other things you could be doing with your spare time that have anywhere near that kind of earning potential.

What's more, eBay doesn't care who you are, where you live, or what you look like: some PowerSellers are very old, or very young. Some live out in the middle of nowhere where selling on eBay is one of the few alternatives to farming or being very poor. eBay tears down the barriers to earning that the real world constantly puts up. There's no job interview and no commuting involved - if you can post things, you can do it. Put it this way: if you know where to get something reasonably cheaply that you could sell, then you can sell it on eBay - and since you can always get discounts for bulk at wholesale, that's not exactly difficult. Buy a job lot of something in-demand cheaply, sell it on eBay, and you're making money already, with no set-up costs.

If you want to dip your toe in the water before you commit to actually buying anything, then you can just sell things that you've got lying around in the house.

Search through that cupboard of stuff you never use, and you'll probably find you've got a few hundred dollars' worth of stuff lying around in there! This is the power of eBay: there is always someone who wants what you're selling, whatever it might be, and since they've come looking for you, you don't even need to do anything to get them to buy it.

5 HARNEESSING COOL CASH FROM EBAY PLATFORM

EBay is becoming the Microsoft of online commerce and you can profit from it. With over 40,000 people signing up every day on eBay there is a trend taking shape that you can take advantage of. Just as Microsoft established its Windows platform as the operating system of choice for 95% of all personal computers, eBay is establishing itself as the gateway to ecommerce for the next century. What's in it for you? Besides the obvious opportunities you have to participate directly on eBay.com there are multiple other ideas that you can capitalize on.

Here are five make money selling on eBay ideas I came up with to help you brainstorm...

1 - Start an eBay club in your community.

Chances are there are MANY people in your area who would attend and you could benefit in many ways. For example, you could become a consultant who teaches others to sell on eBay.

If you are currently part of such a club please let me know. Actually that topic would probably make a great eBook! You could call it, "How to profit by running an eBay club in your neighborhood".

2 - Do what one San Francisco based business is doing and open up an eBay consignment shop.

In March of 2003 a company named AuctionDrop opened its first store.

The company advertised itself as a "drop off" eBay sales center. EBay corporate wasn't involved financially in any way with the launch, but they did provide a lot of help and information showing that they are firmly behind the consignment sales concept.

3 - The world needs a "what's it worth on eBay" toll-free phone service.

SOMEONE needs to start this business. I'll use it! Feel free to steal my idea... just mention me as your inspiration if you do!!

Here's how it would work:

An eBay fanatic like you or me is at a flea market and we come across a box of widgets priced to sell! We think that these widgets would do GREAT on eBay, but we aren't sure. We call the toll-free "what's it worth on eBay" line and we speak to a live person with a fast Internet connection who can tell us what similar items have sold for recently on eBay. They also access other discount shopping pages on the web if necessary to determine the "eBay value" of the item in question.

Using the camera built into your phone you could even submit the image of the widgets to the analyst who is assisting you if it helps them determine the value.

4 - Have a programming idea that will make the lives of eBay buyers or sellers easier?

These products are a HOT market! I am personally approached weekly with one or two new ideas that blow my mind. If you aren't a programmer you can "rent-a-nerd" from sites like elance.com or freelancersdirect.com.

Have the expert make your idea come to life.

That's how PayPal got started! They tried to make the lives of eBay buyers and sellers easier and eventually eBay bought them for MILLIONS (sounds like Microsoft right?)

5 - Become an eBay GURU.

There are only a handful of eBay "experts" on the web. Sure there are a lot of eBooks by anonymous authors who tell you things you could read for yourself on the eBay help menus, but there are very few true experts who make a full-time living teaching others the true insider information that helps eBay sellers tap into the full potential of eBay.

If you follow the Microsoft model for a moment with me you'll see my point here. In the mid 1980's there were only a handful of Microsoft consultants and programmers. Now they are in demand and the good ones are VERY WEALTHY.

With over 40,000 people jumping on eBay every day I promise you that there is a HUGE demand for one-on-one consulting and assistance.

EBay's help menu is good, but I am living proof that people don't rely solely on eBay.com to learn about running an eBay business to make money.

Here's where to start:

Sell and buy on eBay! Learn the basics and then listen to your customers.

Ask them how you can help. Odds are many will want to know how to sell on eBay. Spend some time thinking "BIG PICTURE" about eBay. The opportunities on eBay go far beyond simply running some auctions and earning a few extra bucks.

6 FIND YOUR NICHE ON EBAY

You've spent a day or maybe two or three cruising around eBay. You even registered and bought that iPod skin your niece wants for her birthday. Now it's time to get down to business; that is, your business.

Just exactly what is it that you are going to sell on eBay? The right choice of product is one of the most important decisions you will make when you become an eBay seller. If you are already successfully selling products in a different environment, it is still important to select that perfect product from among your wares that is best suited to your eBay audience.

It is true that many people clean out their closets and turn a tidy penny auctioning off their loot on eBay. However, the day is long past when any moldy old pair of shoes from the back of the closet would be snapped up by an eager eBay buyer. Even if you did make a killing with last year's snow boots, the detritus from your storage unit doesn't make for much of a business plan. There are many people though who have built eBay businesses selling the contents of other people's closets for them so that is one area at which you might want to look.

When considering your product, think along these lines:

Do you want to sell an item which reflects a personal passion? Hobbies are the basis for many eBay success stories as are personal

23

interests such as a specific period in history or a style in fashion.

Do you want to serve as a conduit for other people to sell their products on eBay? Stores to which individuals consign their items are mushrooming throughout the country. This sort of eBay store, however, can be both labor and capital intensive. You will also need to have a solid knowledge base of eBay expertise or employ someone who has the knowhow.

Do you want to expand your current bricks and mortar customer base by establishing an eBay presence?

eBay is an excellent way to quickly implement an online strategy.

Do you want to purchase items and resell them on eBay? You can accomplish this goal by purchasing single pieces that you scout out or by being a drop ship merchant. Picking up wholesale lots is another way of being a reseller.

Now you are well on your way to discovering your route to eBay success.

Once you have narrowed down possibilities for the kind of eBay merchant you want to be, it is time to do more online research. It may seem to you that a lot of time is being spent just looking around and getting a feel for the terrain. You will find though that tomorrow's eBay success is founded on today's eBay research.

7 NEVER LOSE A SELL

How many times have you seen terms similar to this at the end of a listing while browsing eBay? "Terms and Conditions! Please read before bidding". Payment must be made within 48 hours, if payment is not made within this time negative feedback will be left and eBay will be informed.

No new users. If your feedback is below 10 please contact me before bidding or I will retract your bid.

No time wasters, scammers or fraudsters... Why do people do this? It's not going to stop nonpaying bidders, fraudsters or scammers. What it is going to do is result in fewer sales.

Sure, we all hate the non-payers and eBay is a scammer's paradise but do you really think having terms like that is going to stop it? Of course not.

"Payment must be made within 48 hours, if payment is not made within this time negative feedback will be left and eBay will be informed".

If you even hint at giving me negative feedback for any reason I will simply move on to the next auction. You have just lost a sale.

"No new users. If your feedback is below 10 please contact me before bidding or I will retract your bid".

Why pick on the newbie, we all have to start on zero feedback and most of us start by buying something. By having a silly statement like that you could have lost a customer for life.

"No time wasters, scammers or fraudsters".

Do you really think this will stop a fraudster or a scammer?

What I am trying to say here is try and make your buyers experience as pleasant and easy as possible.

For me silly terms like this sound negative and if I can get the product elsewhere I simply close the page and move on to the next auction.

We can all have unpleasant experiences from time to time on eBay and it's not nice if you get scammed but don't take it out on the rest of the eBay community. I would suggest you browse your listings and take a good look at your terms and conditions and if you have any negativity in your auctions have a serious think about changing them as all you are doing is harming your own sales.

All you need to do is keep your terms simple and easy to understand and you will have more sales, guaranteed.

8 THE SECRET POWER OF AN AUCTION TITLE

I get frequent emails from my newsletter readers wondering why their eBay auctions aren't working.

You might have the most brilliant auction description page with a fantastic set of pictures offering a superb item at an incredible price. But the page counter shows after seven days of your auction that it's only been seen by 3 people.

Has that happened to any of your auctions?

If it has, I always start at the same point.

The auction title.

In 99% of cases, the reason for low viewing figures is that your auction title isn't smart enough.

Here are a few facts. At the end of this small list you'll understand the secret power of eBay auction titles... a) 79 million times each day buyers use eBay's search box to locate items in which they are interested... b) eBay's standard search system takes the search words keyed in, and compares them with the titles in its database of 10 million auctions. (Note it doesn't compare them with sub-titles, nor auction descriptions) c) If an auction title doesn't contain the words keyed into the search box, the auction won't get returned in the search list. And that's another of the 79 million searches you've missed out on! d) If an auction isn't returned in a search list, it can't be clicked on to have the auction description viewed.

So, the whole of eBay's default search system relies on matching keywords with auction titles. And that's the secret power of auction titles.

If your title contains words which the buyer searches upon, your auction will be returned time and again in search return lists.

Actually, that's not quite everything. Let's say you want to create a new auction. Your auction title has three functions: 1) To contain keywords. (Number one on this list for the reason you now know!) 2) To persuade buyers to click through to your auction description page 3) To convey what the item is

To decide on the keywords to use, you have to think like a buyer. What words would be used by a person interested in searching for an item like yours? At this stage, just list them. Don't put the words into a sentence yet. Spend as long as you like on this exercise. The more effective you are with this, the less likely you are to have one of those sleepy auctions that rarely get a visitor.

Having listed as many keywords as you can think of, you have to decide which are the strongest. Remember, you only have 55 precious characters for your auction title.

Taking your best keywords, you now create your auction title. It's not an English exam, so it doesn't matter if it doesn't scan like a sentence.

You can add a power word or two if you've space. By this I mean words like stunning, limited edition, unique, rare, new, one-off, exclusive, distinctive, dramatic etc. These are words which can influence buyers to click through to your auction description. They won't be searched on by buyers, so use them sparingly. For the same reason, I don't advocate the use of "clever" words like l@@k or w0w! Finally, do the words in your title convey what the item is? If so, that's it.

You've created a powerful and compelling auction title. And your title will appear more often in search return lists. And, as you know, that's the key!

If you can get your auction to appear more frequently in search return lists, more buyers will view your auction description page.

The more people that visit your auction description page, the more likely you are to make a sale at an acceptable price.

Now you know the secret power, why not create a new title today for one of your auctions? If you do, believe me you'll get your fair share of the 79 million eBay daily searchers.

9 BECOME AN EBAY POWERSELLER TODAY

PowerSeller status is something that many eBay sellers strive to achieve, but few actually manage. With PowerSeller status you gain recognition, respect, and trust which indirectly lead to increased sales. In this article I outline the methods I feel are the best in order to become a PowerSeller.

To qualify for PowerSeller status you have to meet eBay's requirements which are:

1. To uphold the eBay community values, including honesty, timeliness and mutual respect.

2. To sell on average a minimum of $750 (or the exchange rate equivalent) or 100 items per month, for three consecutive months. In order to qualify you need to sell at least 4 items per month.

3. To achieve an overall Feedback rating of 100, of which 98% or more is positive.

4. To have been an active member for 90 days.

5. To have an account in good financial standing.

6. To not violate any severe policies in a 60-day period.

7. To not violate three or more of any eBay policies in a 60-day period.

8. To maintain a minimum of four average monthly listings for the past three months.

Now looking at the above list, I feel points 2, 3, and 8 are the most significant. Points 1, 5, 6, and 7 can be achieved largely by just reviewing and following eBay's rules.

Point 4 is beyond your control, you simply have to accept that the minimum period (from registration with eBay) that you can become a PowerSeller within is 90 days.

However, points 2, 3, and 8 are fully within your control and these are the true keys to becoming an eBay PowerSeller.

I will begin with point 2, which states that you must meet either eBay's Sales Value requirements or eBay's Sales Volume requirements. In my opinion meeting the Sales Volume requirements is much more achievable than meeting the Sales Value requirements, especially when you are just starting out. As it states above, if you achieve sales in excess of 100 units for three months, then you will become a PowerSeller.

Now 100 sales per month may sound a lot for a first time eBook seller, but if you break it down into daily sales then it is only 3-4 sales per day, a much more achievable target. If you run 10 auctions per day and 35% of these are successful then you will be selling enough to qualify for PowerSeller status. If 10 auctions does not bring you the required sales then keep experimenting till you discover the right amount of auctions to achieve 3-4 sales per day.

By following the above instructions you will also fulfill eBay's minimum monthly listing requirement (point 8). That just leaves point 3, which outlines eBay's feedback requirements for becoming a PowerSeller. If you are selling 3-4 items per day (as I outline above) then in three months you will have made approximately 300 sales. From these 300 sales you can potentially receive 300 positive feedback ratings. So long as you maintain a good level of customer service, describe your eBooks accurately within your listings, delivery your eBooks quickly, and promptly respond to customer queries, then you should receive at least 98% positive feedback from these 300 sales.

So to summarize if you want to become an eBay PowerSeller then: • Sign up as an eBay User: -

 If you haven't signed up for a basic eBay account then you should do so.

• Sign up as an eBay Seller: - Once you have a basic eBay account you then need to sign up as a seller.

• Review and Follow eBay's Rules: - In order to become a PowerSeller you must be in good standing with eBay.

• Sell 3-4 eBooks per Day: - Start by listing 10 eBook auctions per day and measure how many are successful. Through testing you can determine how many auctions you need to run in order to generate 3-4 sales per day.

• Maintain a Good Level of Customer Service: - Deliver your eBooks promptly, respond to customer queries quickly, describe your eBooks accurately etc, and you should have no trouble gaining at least 98%+ positive feedback.

• Keep following the above steps for 90 days: - Do the above and you will be a PowerSeller within 90 days, with at least 300 sales to your name, and at least 300 positive feedbacks.

And that's all there is to it. By following eBay's rules, selling 3-4 items per day, and being good to your customers, then you can become a PowerSeller in as little as 90 days from now. Take action today and three months from now you could be rewarded with eBay PowerSeller status.

10 21 SUCCESS STRATEGIES OF POWERSELLERS

The online auction giant - eBay - has exploded on the Internet scene.

Currently boasting over 47 million members, eBay is one of the most visible and far-reaching Internet companies in existence, with a large segment of the population either using the service, or at the very least, aware of it.

Among eBay sellers, there's a designation given to approximately 4% of them.

These are eBay's "PowerSellers", a group of auction sellers that is distinguished by the amount of volume they produce.

The entry-level PowerSeller, the Bronze level, does at least $2,000 a month in eBay sales, maintains a 99% positive feedback level and maintains their eBay account current. Higher award levels are granted at the $10,000 level, (Silver level) and at the $25,000 level. (Gold level) What are some of the strategies and techniques these PowerSellers use?

An eBay PowerSeller is serious - PowerSellers treat their eBay business just like they would any other business. They are dead-serious about it. Look at any Power seller operation and you'll find organized systems and "assembly-line" techniques being used. While a PowerSeller may not have invested thousands of dollars into her operation, she treats it as if she has.

eBay Power sellers are focused - A PowerSeller is focused on listing, packing and shipping, often on different days of the week. Their focus is as intense as that of a Corporate Executive or an Olympic athlete, because they are juggling various activities at the same time.

PowerSellers are organized - The Power seller is organized, otherwise they wouldn't make it to the level of PowerSeller.

Since PowerSellers do a huge volume of listing, packing and shipping each month, they must develop processes to ensure that the items sold are delivered within a reasonable period of time and that customer satisfaction is always at the forefront.

eBay PowerSellers delegate - Power sellers delegate because they have to! Their volume dictates that they hire an assistant to do some of the more repetitive tasks that don't require the Power seller's attention.

This way the PowerSeller can focus on the important money-making tasks of product acquisition and marketing.

Power sellers use assembly line techniques - The PowerSeller has developed smooth running systems to make sure that product fulfillment is accomplished as quickly and efficiently as possible. This may involve setting up a large 4' by 8' table with bubble wrap and packing materials at one end, products in the middle, and boxes, labels and packing tape at the far end.

eBay PowerSellers use Dutch auctions - Many Power sellers have graduated from selling one-of-a-kind knick-knacks found at yard sales and are now selling a volume of the same item through Dutch auctions. In a Dutch auction, a seller can place a large number of the same item up for sale.

The bidders can bid on one or more of the item, but the highest bidders will be first in line to actually get or "win" the products they bid on. So there is a possibility that if someone bid too low, they might not get a product. A PowerSeller uses Dutch auctions often because it is a huge time-saver. This is a true "assembly line" auction from start to finish. The packing and shipping goes a lot faster when the same item is being packed and shipped over and over again.

Power sellers do efficient work - Another trait of the PowerSeller is that they are extremely efficient, knowing that time is money.

A Dutch auction is a great example of this efficiency. In the same period of time that it takes to list one item, you are listing dozens, or even hundreds of items!

This time-efficiency is a powerful way to leverage your time and profits.

eBay PowerSellers "Bulk List" their auctions - Bulk listing your auctions using a bulk listing software or auction management service will dramatically organize your time and allow your eBay operation to run a lot more smoothly.

Having clear There are various options in this area, from eBay's own "Mister Lister" to Blackthorn software to Andale, and Auction Watch auction management services, there are a lot of options for you to look into. These services allow you to list your auctions at your leisure and then schedule them to go live on a certain day and time. This saves you the hassle of having to list your auctions on the particular day that you want them to go up.

Powersellers use clearly focused photos - Power sellers have acquired their status by using clear photos or scans of the items they are selling and making sure that the photos show all flaws. In effect, along with all of the other skills they have acquired, they have also become semi-pro photographers! Many have built a "mini-studio" with optimum lighting and background that is available at their beck and call for those quick shots when they need to e-mail an additional photo to a bidder. The PowerSeller usually has both a Digital Camera for photographing 3-dimensional items and large items and also has a scanner for the paper items and flat items.

Power sellers use headlines with key words and no fluff - A

PowerSeller resists the temptation to use "fluff" words like "L@@K", "WOW" and "MUST SEE". Instead, the PowerSeller uses descriptive words in the headline, realizing that the headline is the "ad for the ad".

A PowerSeller is also "search engine savvy", realizing that keywords in the headline are picked up by the eBay search engine. They are sure to load the headline with descriptive, keywords that help the bidder determine if the item is what they're looking for and keeps out the "fluff".

PowerSellers write thorough and detailed item descriptions – A PowerSeller has achieved their level by maintaining a high ratio of positive feedback. This is primarily accomplished by and accurate descriptions of the items so that the bidder can clearly "imagine" the item as if it were sitting in front of her.

The art of writing a great item description involves an interesting mix of using "selling words" (such as "beautiful", "fantastic", "intricately designed", "gorgeous", "spectacular", "powerful", "colorful", etc.) along with describing the flaws in the item.

A great description should entice the bidder to bid while at the same time providing full and complete disclosure of the item's condition. Your test of whether you have a great description or not is if it answers the following two questions well:

A. If I was to compare the description to the item, while holding the item in my hand, would it be an extremely accurate description? Or would I have good reason to return the item?

B. Does this description entice me to place a bid on the item?

eBay Power sellers give "Benefit of the doubt" customer service - Customer service is such a clichéd catchphrase in American Business today. In the eBay auction world, it is mandatory that you implement a very meticulous level of customer service. PowerSellers have a clear reflection of their level of customer service in their feedback profile. One glance at any eBay seller's feedback profile and you have an instant snapshot of that individual's customer service rating. (Imagine if regular "brick and mortar" stores had a feedback rating posted at the front door!)

This public feedback rating is both your best advertisement (if you provide great customer service) and can also be your downfall. (If you don't) A PowerSeller is constantly aware of this "sign at the front door" and places a high priority on giving stellar customer service.

I call it "Benefit of the doubt" customer service because even in those instances where the customer is clearly wrong, the PowerSeller doesn't argue or get into an emotional "war of words", she simply refunds the money or reduces the shipping cost or sends an unexpected gift with the package. The PowerSeller realizes that business and ego don't mix, they leave their ego on the table - they go on to build lifetime customer relationships.

PowerSellers have their own websites - A PowerSeller realizes that business conditions change. On the Internet, business conditions can change literally from quarter to quarter! Because of the transient and high-speed nature of change in the Internet business, the PowerSeller realizes the value of having their own storefront on the web. They have either built a website themselves or have had someone build a site for them. They have developed a following and a customer base through their eBay auctions that can help sustain them even if dramatic changes come about on their main selling venue. As eBay continues to evolve and change - applying restrictive and invasive policies - this will become more of a priority for all eBay sellers, not just Power sellers.

An eBay PowerSeller makes it easy for bidders to pay - By offering a variety of payment options, Power s ellers make it easy for winning bidders to pay for their items. They offer to accept Checks, Money Orders, all types of credit and debit cards through PayPal, Billpoint, or their own Merchant Accounts. By offering a wide variety of payment options, they open up their market of available bidders and end up with higher ending bids as a result.

Powersellers offer discounts on multiple items - Whether it is a discount on shipping multiple items or a discount on the actual price of multiple items, PowerSellers realize the value of a good customer and treat that customer special.

Unexpected discounts tell the customer "You're special" and build a reciprocity that keeps customers coming back or searching the PowerSellers' auctions. PowerSellers are always on the lookout for great deals - The PowerSeller is the consummate "deal-maker". Whether it's at an antique store or at a swap meet, the Power seller is always thinking about things they can re-sell.

They find that pop-culture collectible and buy it. List it the same day and see the bid amount grow and grow. Part of the thrill of selling on eBay is "taking a shot" and listing items that you are not familiar with. Seeing the items shoot up in price is a fun and enjoyable hobby!

PowerSellers are always on the lookout for great deals – The PowerSeller is the consummate "deal-maker". Whether it's at an antique store or at a swap meet, the PowerSeller is always thinking about things they can re-sell. They find that pop-culture collectible and buy it. List it the same day and see the bid amount grow and grow. Part of the thrill of selling on eBay is "taking a shot" and listing items that you are not familiar with. Seeing the items shoot up in price is a fun and enjoyable hobby!

An eBay PowerSeller does not mind making money! - A PowerSeller has no "issues" with making money. Many Americans have been brought up with the notion that the only "respectable way" of making money is by working at a job for thirty years. Sales and selling is looked down upon.

The PowerSeller is way beyond that. They have a healthy attitude towards making money and it becomes like a "hobby" to them! As new and strange as it may appear to the more traditional types, selling on eBay is one of the easiest and most lucrative ways to make a part-time income.

The alternatives to selling on eBay are either too time consuming or too unrealistic. This "new" way of earning an income is powerful and realistic.

eBay PowerSellers enjoy their work-at-home lifestyle – PowerSellers love the fact that they get to work from home while the rest of America sits on the freeway, waiting for their fellow "worker-bees" to move. The freedom of having a Home Based Business is something the Power seller relishes and appreciates. This enjoyment of the lifestyle has many tangible benefits - better health, freedom of time, being able to spend more quality time with kids, attending their school functions and field trips, better scheduling of time (around the rush hours) and an overall feeling of well-being. There is no doubt; working from home is the wave of the future.

Power sellers are willing to invest in their business - Whether it

means investing in a high-speed cable modem or DSL connection, high quality computer components, including digital cameras, monitors, keyboards, etc. or whether it means buying a "Featured Auction" listing which will drive further traffic to their other auctions, the PowerSeller knows how to use their money wisely. There is a difference between wasting money and investing money in your business.

An eBay PowerSeller knows when to "invest" money into their business. Basically, anything that saves you time or saves you money is an investment in your business. As an example: A digital camera is a huge time-saver over taking traditional 35 mm photos and then scanning them.

The investment in a digital camera is one of the best ways to become a more efficient eBay seller! A PowerSeller stays up-to-date on auction trends and changes - Because Power sellers take their business seriously, they constantly keep themselves up to date on the latest industry trends and changes. They do this by buying books about online auctions, participating in eBay Message Boards/Forums, and staying tuned to the eBay Announcements Board.

They don't want to be caught off guard with a new change or new policy that might affect their business.

An eBay PowerSeller is always looking for better ways to do things - Whether it's listing auctions, packing and shipping, getting organized, or expanding their business, Power sellers are always looking to improve their online business. This is the nature of all successful business people; they want to improve their business constantly. As the 4% of eBay sellers known as PowerSellers continue to improve their processes, here's hoping that the above strategies will be helpful reminders in improving yours!

11 WHAT YOU CAN SELL ON EBAY

One of the reasons why sellers and buyers love to use eBay so much is the ability to sell anything. Whatever it is that buyers are looking for they are almost guaranteed to find it on eBay. That's why there is currently over 100 million eBay members.

There have been some unusual items sold on eBay. Some items that sellers have considering throwing out actually fetch a substantial amount of money, just because for some reason or another someone else in the world wanted it. This opens up a huge market for anyone considering entering the eBay selling business. It almost gives you a license to source anything and then to sell it on eBay.

Note that although eBay provides the opportunity to sell almost anything, it will now allow illegal items, animals (including animals that were once alive, and are now stuffed and mounted), replicas, alcohol, weapons and firearms, tobacco products, prescription or illegal drugs, or services to be sold.

There are also several items that you may think are fine to sell, although they are in fact against eBay selling policies. Items such as tickets may be sold, but it is illegal to sell tickets for a higher price than you originally paid for them. This is called ticket scalping, and it is illegal.

Copyrighted items - such as DVD's, CD's, or software - may not be sold through eBay auctions. However, CD's, DVD's or any software that you bought legitimately can be sold as long as they are not copies that you have made. If you are unsure as to whether you are allowed to sell any particular item, contact eBay before going ahead and listing the item or sourcing the product.

The problem that many have when wanting to enter the eBay selling business though is that they do not know what and where to find items to sell. This is vital to the success of any eBay seller. You need to keep an eye on your competition and also try and source your products for the cheapest available price.

Small product niches can provide a good revenue stream, although selling in several niches is even better.

Why? Well with the amount of current eBay sellers and future sellers looking to get into eBay selling, it provides the opportunity for large competition in your niche. Selling in several niches means that should competition become too fierce in one of the niches, you still have your other revenue streams to rely upon. The key to successful eBay selling is finding a large quantity of products for the cheapest available price.

12 WHAT YOU CAN'T SELL ON EBAY

eBay is the Internet's largest marketplace with hundreds of items of all kinds and varieties being sold every day. However, there are some things that are prohibited from being sold on eBay.

Selling any of these prohibited items on eBay can lead to your account being terminated. In some cases, you may even face criminal charges.

Here are the prohibited items:

1. No wildlife animals, pets are allowed to be sold on eBay. This is really due to animal conservation laws and offenders may face prosecution.

2. No fake or counterfeit currencies may be sold on eBay

3. Any kind of downloadable media. This usually refers to any video, software and any digital media items. There are exceptions in this case which is if you hold the copyright or the sole owner of the item. All others are in violation of the eBay vero program. Do note, you may be asked by eBay to verify your copyright ownership, trademark, etc., if you sell it on eBay.

4. School Related Software. This means any school related software that is being sold at a reduced pricing to student and researchers.

5. This is similar to point 3 except it deals with copyright, trademark, etc.

Examples include brand names of popular consumer products. Beta software, CD, VCD and DVD material in which there is no proof of authenticity.

6. Prohibited Goods from other countries cannot be sold on eBay 7. Names, faces, signatures of people without their proper permission 8. You can't sell any kind of weapons or ammunition on eBay 9. You can't sell any government documents or personal documents such as identification card, passport, car license etc.

13 BARGAIN SOURCES FOR AUCTION RESALE

We all have seen the ads and infomercials on TV, hawking their eBay reseller kits and proclaiming how many people make substantial incomes off of eBay. Is it possible? Yes, there are quite a few people out there that their entire income source is derived from auctions like eBay and Yahoo auctions. Is it easy and where do they get their items cheap enough to resell on eBay for a big profit? Well, that takes a little delving into.

First you have to identify a product or item that has an immediate demand. It does not matter how good the price you get on something is if no one wants to buy it, right? Scour eBay and you can easily find some hot selling items like Ralph Lauren polo shirts, Dolce & Gabana jeans, almost anything Versace, etc. Jot down these hot items. Do not be like some sellers that sell knock offs incorrectly listed as originals, you may make a quick buck, but will soon be found out and labeled as a scammer and your sales and feedback scores will plummet. It's not worth it. A good score and reputation will make you or break you on eBay.

The best sources may even be local to you. Many eBayers buy items from Marshalls, TJ Maxx, and even their local dollar stores and resell them on eBay.

eBay is a huge market place and the possibilities are limitless. The better the pictures and the more detailed your listings and product descriptions the higher the price you will fetch. You can then grow into bulk. Many companies will sell bulk lots of overruns and extra out of season stuff from clothes to outmoded electronics gear. This is easy, just Google wholesale or bulk lots. Be prepared to buy a lot of 2,000 or so items. You will get a great price break, but so you do not get stuck with 2,000 or more items that no one wants, do your research first.

Proper research is the key to making it big on eBay. If you do not do it, you will not make it. It is that simple. eBay and the internet can make you and they can also break you. Go to advanced search on the upper right hand corner of any eBay web page. On the resulting page look up items that are selling and only look at items that have bids.

You can also click on sellers and see what other items they are selling. This will give you an idea of what is hot and what is not. Also look up completed auctions. This will tell you what specific items are selling for on average and why one sellers listing brings a higher value than another's. Once you have done your research and determined that there is a high demand and good profit potential for an item or two, find a good source for it.

The easiest way to find your sources is to Google the keywords of wholesale, bulk, lots, and their variants along with what you are looking for. You will be surprised at what you find. Yes, you will have to weed through a lot of sites that are incorrectly listed and junk sites, but that is the nature of the internet. If it were too easy, everyone would be doing it. There is a little work and risk involved like the best prices and highest profits involve huge bulk orders and if you do not do your research correctly you could be left with a huge order and no sales.

I cannot say this enough research it thoroughly. If you do not believe me on this, just look up wholesale or bulk lots on eBay. Most of the listings you will find are from people that bought bulk without proper research and are just trying to unload their bad buy or investment and cut their losses. Sometimes these listings can turn out to be gold also as they may not have properly listed or displayed their items and that in itself can be the difference between a big PowerSeller and a want to be.

Take it from me, I am one of the original eBay PowerSellers since 1996 and research and properly displayed listings with high feedback ratings are the key to making it big on eBay, regardless what items or category you select.

14 BREAKDOWN OF EBAY AUCTIONS

Most people consider starting a business of their own at some point during their lives. With all of the opportunities there are for making money online these days, it easy to get started. Regardless of whether you want to sell products or provide services, eBay is a great place to test the online retail waters.

There is a casual, almost garage-sale-like, atmosphere to eBay, but don't let that fool you, eBay is big business. There are over 750,000 people making their fulltime living on eBay. If you are considering become one of them, then you have to enter into this arena, fully prepared to win. The first step in getting started with an eBay business is to become familiar with the eBay website. Spend some time getting to know the environment.

If you don't already have an eBay account, open one up. Once you have a registered account you can begin to make small purchases. By purchasing small items you minimize your risk while learning how this ecommerce giant operates, while at the same time building up your positive feedback.

Whether you ultimately want to be a seller or just mainly a buyer, going through the entire life-cycle of an auction will help you see all the various facets of planning, initiating and following through with a sale on eBay.

There are eight steps in the eBay auction life cycle.

1. Prospective buyer registers to sell. Before a seller can begin selling items on eBay they must register. The registration process is easy and only requires you to put in basic information about yourself.

2. Registered buyer searches for and finds seller's item. A good title with appropriate, descriptive key words will help a perspective buyer find a seller's items during the search.

3. Buyer enters a bid large enough to beat out other bidders and win sellers item. Since eBay has a proxy bidding system a bidder can enter the highest bid they feel comfortable placing right at the start of the bidding process.

Note that the highest bid a buyer places will only be used if there is competition with other bidders that forces the bid up, if there is no competition for the item the bid will not increase, regardless of the highest proxy bid entered.

4. The buyer initiates payment to the seller through PayPal, check or money order. eBay owns PayPal and as such PayPal is the easiest way to make payments online. Over 85% of all eBay transactions use PayPal.

5. Seller packs the item and ships. Breakage in shipping is one of the biggest reasons for returns on eBay. It pays to spend the extra time and expense for bubble wrap, strong boxes, and packing tape, to ensure that an item arrives intact.

6. Buyer receives package. Delivery confirmation and package tracking allow both buyer and seller to be aware of when the package arrives.

7. Positive feedback left by both parties. If the seller accurately describes the item, listing the item with lots of pictures, charges actual shipping costs, packages the item, and ships promptly, they will more than likely have a happy buyer. If the buyer pays promptly, uses PayPal, and leaves the seller positive feedback, the buyer will more

than likely make the seller happy. When both parties are happy they usually trade positive feedback.

As you can see the process of understanding ecommerce on eBay is easy, you just have to be familiar with the rules of the game. Videos providing in-depth tutorials of this series of eBay Selling Strategies are available at no cost at eBay Selling Basics.

15 5 SIMPLE STEPS TO BUILDING YOUR EBAY BUSINESS

eBay is a website where people from all over the world come to buy and sell their products in an auction style format and it has become one of the largest and well known online auction sites in the world. It opens up an opportunity for people to earn money from the comfort of their very own home and improve the lifestyle they have.

There are over one hundred thousand people making their full time living on eBay and there are probably millions of people that are making a nice supplementary income from it. Trading on eBay just comes down to good business sense and professionalism. You can build a business using eBay and you can make your full-time living from eBay but first you should study and learn how things work and what works best.

In this article, I am going to cover five things that you should know and always implement in your eBay auction business in order to make it more efficient and effective.

1) Find a Hot Market. One of the most common mistakes made by new eBay sellers is believing they have a hot selling product but not knowing for sure. This is a very bad idea and could lose you a lot of money. You should always research and find out what products are selling well and find a way for you to provide those products to buyers. You can find hot markets by simply surfing eBay's finished items and seeing if there are regular sales of a product. You can also find ways to provide those products via wholesalers and drop shippers.

2) Study Your Markets Competitors. When you have a hot selling

product then you should study other eBay sellers that are selling the same product and see how they run their business. This is an excellent way to do a number of things such as finding who the top sellers are, learning how they do things, finding ways you can improve your business and just basically finding out what works and what doesn't.

You should always know your competitors and know why they are successful. Then you can simply implement what they do in your own eBay auction business.

3) Over Deliver. When trading on eBay it is very easy to get lost in the crowd and lose your customers to other sellers and that is why you must over deliver. By over deliver I mean delivering extra value in your service and making your service more efficient, friendlier and more appealing for your customers. You can do things like providing extra gifts and bonuses with your products, sending your products first class and as soon as you receive payment, providing phone support and other little things that will make a big difference to your long term success.

4) Be Professional. On eBay you will find that some people are just impossible to deal with. They will cause you all sorts of problems, never be pleased no matter what you do, leave you terrible feedback and things like that but you must not let these people affect how you run your business. When someone does something to you that is completely inappropriate, it can be very tempting to tell them what you think of them but you shouldn't. You must always maintain your professionalism even if it is being tested to extreme levels.

5) Continue to Learn and Tweak Your Business. There are always new things that people can learn. Even the most successful people

can learn new things, so you should always be looking out for things that you can use in your business to make it better and always try to improve your eBay auction business.

16 BENEFITS OF STARTING AN EBAY BUSINESS

Selling on eBay is becoming more and more popular. One of the reasons for this is the many benefits that come with selling online using a secure and reputable company such as eBay.

eBay appeals to buyers because:

• They are looking for bargains that they can find in one place, in this case a virtual marketplace.

• They are looking for hard to find items.

• They are looking for items that they collect.

The first benefit of selling at eBay is that you have very little to lose. There are no start-up costs at eBay and this means that you are not risking any of your money to start a new money-making project. You can get started quickly with very little investment. Investment on your part is limited to the products you are selling and the minimal fee that eBay charges you for listing your items.

You can sell on eBay in your spare time. This means that you can keep your full time job and make extra money on the side. You can determine how much or how little time you want to invest in selling items on eBay. You will be able to work from your own home, from anywhere in the world where you have an Internet connection. There is no need for you to have your own website. eBay does all of the Internet hosting for you.

This is perfect for stay-at-home parents who want to earn money while staying home with their children. You can start selling with absolutely no marketing experience. When you list your sellable items at eBay you can be certain that buyers are coming to you. All you have to do is create an eBay listing for your item that is catchy and makes buyers read it twice.

Be accurate and concise when creating the description for your items. More information is better than not enough information. Giving buyers the opportunity to ask you questions about the item you are selling is an important technique that you should use consistently.

Using a virtual marketplace to sell your items means that you don't have to take your sellable items to an auction house or flea market to make extra money. It can be time consuming and exhausting to haul your items back and forth in your attempt to sell them. eBay is simple and easy to use. Once you sell one or two items you will become more and more confident with the way the selling process works.

eBay is designed to make the process of selling your items as easy and uncomplicated as possible while at the same time working in a seamless and successful fashion. Help at eBay is always close at hand so you never have to wait if you require assistance. There are many other benefits of using eBay to sell items. The key factor is that it all comes down to your personal preferences. You are in control of what you sell and the manner in which you are going to sell it. You are the one who decides how much effort and time you invest in the business of online e-commerce.

17 SUCCESS ON EBAY

Everyone has heard incredible stories of people making big money on eBay selling stuff from their attic or "junk" they pick up at garage sales. While these stories make the most skeptical of us tingle at the thought of easy money, hard work and determination are the key words for selling on eBay.

She has written the following advice for those of you who are serious about making a profit with eBay.

1. FOCUS - Choose something to sell that you already know about; preferably something that you love! When you are already familiar with an item, you don't waste time wondering whether it will sell or how much you should pay for it.

My experience with garage sale shopping and hoping that I picked things that people wanted to buy was a total flop because I didn't know what I was looking for. I ended up with piles of stuff that I couldn't sell and wasted lots of time looking for garage sales. Those of you, who have done this, know the total frustration of a wasted Saturday morning.

2. RESEARCH - The other option is to research on eBay what is already selling and then find a cheap source of that item. Garage sales are a good way to find stuff if you already know what you are looking for. Call ahead to garage sales that are listed in the paper and ask if they have what you are looking for. Don't waste your time and gas poking around town

looking for sales that don't have what you want! Garage sales work best if you know a lot about antiques or collectibles. These items sell well on eBay, but they only work for people who know what they are looking for and how much antiques and collectibles are worth.

Other things that sell well on eBay are items that have a model number or item number or an ISBN number (this is for eBay's sister site Half.com which lists books by ISBN numbers - this is great for selling old textbooks or out of print items!) People go to eBay looking for deals on electronics, brand-name clothes, video games, computers, and software. Things that can be easily identified with words sell well on eBay.

Things that do NOT sell well on eBay are things that don't have a hard and fast description; items that need to be touched or smelled or rely on aesthetics to sell. Home interior items are examples of things that DON'T sell well on eBay.

People who shop eBay are looking for something specific. If they don't already know about what you are selling, they aren't going to just browse eBay's categories looking for your items. Use this as a guide when choosing what to sell.

The best way to find cheap sources for these items is to work out a deal with a wholesaler. This way you get the best possible pricing and you can still make a profit! Because, remember, people shopping eBay are looking for a deal!

3. CONSIDER DROP SHIPPING - This is the best possible method that I have found for making eBay a profitable enterprise. (Unless you are going the route of antiques and collectibles)

Drop shipping eliminates the need for storing your items, packaging, and shipping them. This ate most of the profit that I would have made because it took so much time to do all of this. And most of us don't have an empty room we can devote just for storing stuff for eBay and even if we did, we have to come up with a system for inventory.

You end up with a lot of the headaches that traditional businesses have to deal with. SO, the BEST way that I have found to make eBay profitable for the average person is this:

• Research what is selling on eBay.

• Go to the library and go through a copy of the business directory and find WHOLESALERS that sell the product that eBay goers are looking for.

• Contact the wholesaler and work out a deal with them.

The key is turning strangers into friends and friends into customers!
• Ask for great pricing in exchange for you selling their product as part of the deal, arrange for them to ship directly to your customers.

So, basically, you are acting as a retailer for them. They benefit, by getting sales with no overhead, and you benefit by being able to be competitive on eBay and not having the headaches of storing, packing, and shipping! It is a wonderful win-win agreement! If you do choose the antiques and collectibles route, there are great resources out there to teach you how to do it as profitably as possible.

My favorite is Starting an eBay Business for Dummies. And, as a resource to market your eBay auctions for even better profits, I would definitely recommend Seth Godin's book Permission Marketing. It is a MUST for growing your eBay business and keeping customers coming back to your auctions again and again.

18 DRIVE YOURSELF TO MAKE MORE MONEY

Big ticket items are increasingly popular on eBay. Cars are probably one of the best examples of this. In fact, eBay is the largest dealer of used cars in the USA and eBay's car sales in the UK is also growing significantly. Every 16 seconds, a car is sold on eBay! If you're an eBay seller, here's an idea you might like to consider to make extra cash.

The vast majority of car dealers don't use eBay. They advertise in the press, usually locally, and their customers likewise usually live within reach of the car dealer. What eBay Motors has successfully proved is that people will bid on cars from owners hundreds or even thousands of miles away. Why not take your eBay selling expertise, and offer your services to car dealers in your local area? You know how to create auctions, take and upload photos, and manage auctions. The dealers have vehicles which are getting a tiny fraction of the exposure which eBay could offer.

You might decide to offer this to dealers on a no-cost basis. In other words, you bear the cost of eBay's listing and selling fees. The benefit here is that there is no reason why the dealer shouldn't give you the go ahead. They could get a sale without cost to them and no extra effort on their behalf. That's what I call a no-brainer! Alternatively, you could pass on the fees to the dealer on the basis that they would be spending money anyway on press advertising.

The other commercial arrangements are simple. You could work on a commission, where you get a percentage of the sale price.

Or you could agree a price which the dealer will accept for the sale of the car, and anything you can get above that price is your profit. This would work particularly well if the dealer has had a vehicle for some time, and has no interest in it. The best types of cars to sell on eBay are those that are unusual for one reason or another. It might be vintage or classic vehicles, sports cars or high value models. You're best to avoid what might be termed "normal" cars. It also depends on the kind of dealers you have in your area.

One of the major potential problems is easily handled. You can't expect the dealer to cease trying to sell a vehicle which you have on eBay auction. In every auction you run for a car, you state that the vehicle is also on sale in other ways, and that you reserve the right to withdraw it before the end of the auction period. You will see such statements on many eBay car auctions.

This idea doesn't have to be limited to cars. There are big ticket item opportunities in several categories. You're looking for retail outlets which tend to concentrate on local advertising and local trade. Examples of this would be jewelers, antique traders and real estate operations. With big ticket items, just one or two sales per week could make a significant difference to you.

Worth thinking about!

19 TOP 10 MONEY-MAKING SECRETS

Some people think they can make money on eBay by setting a high price for something they perceive to have a high value. The problem is that their perception is skewed. Very often they assign an emotional value to the item and are disappointed when they can't get their asking price. You can avoid disappointment and even losing money by following these simple eBay selling steps...

1: Don't buy anything...

The object here is to make money on eBay. So don't spend any. It often very tempting to surf eBay and buy something that you think you need. Start out by having a "garage sale" or clean out the basement. In other words sell what you got. On eBay especially, one man's junk is another man's treasure. Old books, toys, tools, souvenirs, office supplies, electronics, etc. Anything you can find, you can sell. You will just have to set reasonable expectations on price.

2: Research pricing...

The biggest mistake made is setting an opening bid too high. It works against you in two ways. First, a prospective bidder may not even open your item. The opening price is listed on the summary. Second, it costs more to list it at a higher price.

3: Lose the sentimental value...

This is the toughest part. When we are selling mementos,

memorabilia or other items, we tend to remember the circumstances upon which we got them. "Remember how long we had to stand in line for those concert tickets?" or "That was from my first car."

If you can't stand to part with it...don't. Other people will not have the same attachment to it that you do. Price it as if you were going to go to the mall and buy it today. Antiques and ephemera generate their own "sentimental value" by the provenance or history of the object. But it is unlikely that your ownership has added much to that.

4: Set a low starting price...

The best opening bid is one that is high enough to indicate some value. Bids starting at a penny or a dollar are often thought of as junk and a waste of time. But a hundred dollar item opening at ten dollars is a real bargain. To determine the best starting bid, surf eBay and the rest of the Internet for similar items. Look at both the new retail cost and the resale value then set your price low enough to generate some excitement. It will rise to its proper value...

5: Place it for 7 days...

This is the standard listing. Listing it for a shorter period may seem to generate a bid sooner. In reality, it is missing out on a lot of potential buyers who will return when it's close to closing time - not the best way to make money on eBay.

6: Make it pretty...

At the very least use a photo. No matter how well you describe you will ALWAYS benefit from the extra "thousand words".

It will result in more bids and higher bids (important to make money on eBay). Even if it looks like junk, the buyer knows exactly what they are getting. Even better, use ad builder software to dress up your presentation.

7: Don't buy any extras...

BOLD listings, slide show, gift tags, etc. all add up to increase the fees associated with your listing. This only serves to reduce your profit.

8: Cover your costs...

Do not estimate the shipping costs. Use actual costs. Be sure to include charges for the shipping materials, as well as postage. The best way is to use free materials supplied for Priority Mail. Using Stamps.com or a postage meter is convenient, but be sure your scale is accurate. More than once I've had to add postage at the post office.

9: Do use PayPal...

The quicker you get paid, the quicker you make money on eBay. PayPal is instantaneous. No waiting for the "check is in the mail" and no waiting for the check to clear.

10: Do it often...

The more you sell, the more money you make on eBay. Don't worry that you only getting a few dollars at a time. Ten dollars a day, every day for a year will get you $3,650. Not a killing, but quite a nice vacation.

20 HOW TO OBTAIN LIFE LONG CUSTOMERS

One concept I try hard to communicate to each of my members is the overall power of eBay and how we can use eBay not only as a way to make sales but also as a way to obtain life-long customers. You can make very good money by simply listing and selling on eBay, given you've got the right product and you're using the right methods.

However, you can make an absurd income on eBay if you use them as not only a "store" but also as a marketing tool...

How do you do this? It's as simple as creating a newsletter you can offer along with your eBay listings. In this article I'm going to briefly cover how you can use a newsletter to do the following:

1. Turn Your eBay Browsers Into Customers

2. Turn eBay Customers Into Life-Long Customers. This article will be a two part lesson. It can be very simple to create a newsletter just by following a few easy steps...

1. Turn Your eBay Browsers Into Customers

Remember that although your initial goal is to turn your eBay "browsers" into buyers, you can't stop there. Many eBay sellers assume if they don't have something the "browser" is looking for, and then they aren't going to sell anything to that person at all. But, that is far from the truth.

You've already overcome the most difficult part, which is getting the "browser" to your listings. The important part is to make sure each visit counts. You have to make sure that once you get a visitor to one of your listings, they don't leave until you have tried everything possible to get their contact information such as name and email, to try and convert them to a future customer.

Let's say you sell home decor products and someone visits your listings while looking for a particular window treatment. The visitor views the auction they were led to and also visits your "other listed items". This particular visitor doesn't find what the item he/she is looking for. So, he/she leaves your auctions and you never have the chance to do business with this person, right? Wrong! It would be very simple to invite each visitor to your About Me page, with something like, "Click here to visit my About Me page and receive free, weekly tips to help you redecorate your home like a professional designer for half the cost."

Once the visitor reaches your About Me page, you can provide them with simple instructions on how they can receive your weekly newsletter for free to get the tips they are looking for. A sound easy doesn't it? It is and, in just minutes, you can have this set up and will be collecting valuable names and email addresses.

2. Turning eBay Customers Into Life-Long Customers

This is so easy, but SO overlooked in the eBay industry. If eBay is your business, then you have to treat it as such. Like any "typical" business, you try to do your best in every aspect of the sale to ensure your customer will return. However, online it is so easy to get lost in the shuffle.

Once you pick up a customer, you need to be sure to stay in contact with that customer so there is no doubt in your mind that, if they return to eBay to purchase something, they will come to you first. There are auction programs such as Vendio that offer great customer management software.

You can easily include a "join my mailing list" link to all of your post-sale emails. Remember, once you sell to an eBay customer, they are your customer so you're allowed to email them off of eBay.

You want to present them with an offer such as, "Join my monthly newsletter and receive updates on my product line including notification of newly listed items, and member discounts." Doing this allows you to stay in touch with your past customers to keep you fresh in their minds.

And it also gives you the opportunity to invite them to your auction listings on a regular basis. But, remember you have to treat your customers well. You have to provide them with good offers so they appreciate you and want to return.

Whether you obtain the names and emails of those who are visiting your auctions, or those who have bought from you, collecting the information of those who are in the market for your type of product is absolutely priceless.

If they are on eBay to purchase a product "like" the products you offer, they are more than likely going to purchase this type of product again in the near future. If you offer them sound information and special discounts, as well as keep in touch with them, chances are they will come to you first for their next purchase.

Good Luck!